INTENTIONAL HOUSE BY MONTH:

A SEASONAL GUIDE TO FAMILY CONNECTION AT HOME

CARLY THORNOCK

Printed in the United States of America.

ISBN 978-0-578-22783-2

www.intentionalhouse.com

FROM ROBERT ANTON WILSON

THE EARTH WILL SHAKE
Volume 1 of the
Historical Illuminatus Chronicles

They have been with us all through history:
The "Invisible College" of wisdom, and their
adversaries—the destroyers—who rise
from the flames to burn again. The history
of the world is their story: a conspiracy as
vast and all-encompassing as the riddle of
time itself.

ISBN 1-56184-162-5

THE WIDOW'S SON
Volume 2 of the
Historical Illuminatus Chronicles

Throughout history, secret societies have
played a crucial role in shaping events that
have created our world. Only an inner circle
of power elite know the full extent of the
influence of the conspiracy...

ISBN 1-56184-063-3

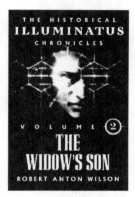

NATURE'S GOD
Volume 3 of the
Historical Illuminatus Chronicles

They are the most secret of organizations
and the most powerful—the Illuminati. They
continue to shift the patterns of history to
fulfill plans of their own, to open pathways
to power which ordinary mortals are never
meant to tread.

ISBN 1-56184-164-1

FROM ROBERT ANTON WILSON

PROMETHEUS RISING

Readers have been known to get angry, cry, laugh, even change their entire lives. Practical techniques to break free of one's 'reality tunnels'. A very important book, now in its *eighth* printing.

"*Prometheus Rising* is one of that rare category of modern works which intuits the next stage of human evolution... Wilson is one of the leading thinkers of the Modern age."
—Barbara Marx Hubbard

ISBN 1-56184-056-4

QUANTUM PSYCHOLOGY
How Brain Software Programs You & Your World

The book for the 21st Century. Picks up where *Prometheus Rising* left off. Some say it's materialistic, others call it scientific and still others insist it's mystical. It's all of these—and none.

Second Revised Edition!

"Here is a Genius with a Gee!"
—Brian Aldiss, *The Guardian*

"What great physicist hides behind the mask of Wilson?"
—*New Scientist*

ISBN 1-56184-071-8

For Chase, Nyle, Gordon, and Eddy, who make all the
seasons entertaining and joyful.

With special thanks to the many editing eyes and to Shera,
for her layout and illustrational genius.

CONTENTS

INTRODUCTION

As a child I loved to sit on the floor in my bedroom and mentally architect secret passages between my room and the kitchen; I also created a floor that retracted to an immense, Beauty-and-the-Beast-style underground personal library filled with leather bound mystery novels and illustrated encyclopedias. I'm sure this comes as no surprise, but I do love a good snack and I really love books. Because of these loves, I wanted to make space for them to surround me, even if the spaces were largely imagined. I drew and I dreamed. I remember that these dreams made me feel adventurous and I craved being taken away with the wonder of countless possibilities.

All too often we find ourselves grown up and craving that sense of adventure, self-directed purpose, and whimsy again. Surprisingly, the answer is not buying a second house on the beach or surviving until retirement to finally feel alive again. Rather, the answer to creating the life you love NOW is merely a perspective shift with a few little tweaks around the house! The adventure and wonder, excitement and connection, purpose and whimsy lies in the power of the everyday, the things we do in and out, in the most basic of places: our homes.

I always knew I wanted to be a designer of homes. I didn't know as a kid that my path would lead me to a degree in Marriage, Family, and Human Development, studying how the house itself can impact family relationships. When I realized that the home can be more than just a pretty place where you spend lots of time and tons of energy cleaning, I was completely hooked! Literally, the way you design and use your house has an impact on your emotional, physical, mental, and relational health!

I can not even wait to share with you the life-changing knowledge I've gleaned from my own personal research and the work of other environmental design and family science experts, all pointing to the fact that our places and spaces matter.

What if I told you that doing dishes could be fun again?!?! AND, what if this working together might just be the ticket to cracking the hard exterior of a struggling teen? Truly, when we see our homes in the right light, we have all that we need to foster meaningful relationships, develop skill sets, refine character, and remember our deepest purposes. To me, this power is unlocked when I remember that every mundane task and action, like washing the dishes or changing diapers, presents an opportunity to connect with my higher purpose and the people in my life.

Thinking like this, striving to find meaning in the mundane, recreates that childhood feeling that something amazing is happening just below the floorboards. I can be doing something seemingly normal on the outside, but inside, mopping floors can transform into team figure skating practice full of laughter and outtakes. I recognize the unknowingly captive audience at my table when little mouths are full-- my children have the lucky opportunity to appreciate my ultra fascinating and morally rich storytelling talents.

A home is made of things functional and things beautiful. When we add in a third element of things "intentional", all of the sudden the functional and classic stove has a deeper purpose of serving life-sustaining food (and love) to the people we care for most.

I might not don't know it all, but I know this: something is definitely happening beneath the floorboards of our homes, and while it may not be a literal library with a retractable ceiling right beneath my bedroom (think "It's A Wonderful Life" swimming pool style) like I dreamed up as a girl, often the things we do have deeper implications than merely the completion of a task.

Each month and each season present us with so many chances to see and seek the beautiful, the good, the true, and each other. This book is an effort to help us be intentional in appreciating what we have and taking advantage of the abundant opportunities for love, joy, and connection that present within our homes and throughout the seasons of the year.

For each month you will find ten thoughts, activities, or challenges that will help you use the season and your home to center yourself and connect with those you love. I suggest that you read through the whole month at once, and then choose a suggestions few to incorporate into your life.

My intention is to get you thinking about all the possibilities that are disguised as chores and routines! I hope you'll find excitement in reinvigorating your to-do list with an eye toward loving those closest to you.

Please write in this book. There is an abundance of intentional white space so that you can add your own thoughts, jokes, recipes, traditions, and inspirations in the margins as they come to you. Make this yours. Use the simple suggestions I offer as a launching point to create the home you've always imagined and the life you love.

Life is truly wonderful, isn't it?

All my best,

Carly

JANUARY

GET GRATEFUL:

Make gratitude part of your lifestyle. Researchers have discovered that a grateful outlook has the potential to have profound emotional and interpersonal benefits (Emmons & McCullough, 2003).

Take ten minutes to appreciate your home. Make a list of why you love it. You can include smells you're fond of, furniture that makes you happy for any reason at all, the functional aspects of your house that keep life running smoothly, or the people that populate your home. Then kiss the list. Happy New Year. (Kissing optional**)

· ·

Gratitude unlocks the fullness of life. It turns what we have into enough, and more. It turns denial into acceptance, chaos to order, confusion to clarity. It can turn a meal into a feast, a house into a home, a stranger into a friend.

- Melody Beattie

· ·

ROUTINE AWARENESS:

Notice how you use your home each morning. Do you do the same things over and over? (For example, get up on the left side of the bed, hit the bathroom automatically, eat breakfast in the same chair, brush teeth starting on the bottom left, get dressed with pants first and sitting on that particular corner of the bed, etc.)

Could you do it blindfolded?

Is there anything you do purely because your house is a certain way?

For instance, I like to wash my dishes at 10 am because that's when the morning sun hits my sink. Soak in all the little routines you execute in your home today.

Are you taking advantage of your home's assets? Are you doing things the way you'd like to be doing them, or is the house dictating your routine for better or for worse (do you normally lean your shoulder into the door to get it to open it or is that an environmental quirk you adopted)? Is there anything that you notice that you'd like to change? What do you absolutely love?

VISION:

What are your resolutions for this new year? How can your house help you remember them? Take a minute and make a sign to remind yourself of one resolution and put it somewhere other than your mirror where you'll see it. Kitchen cupboard? On your computer?

You can also put a token "reminder object" out to remind yourself (a paperclip on a ledge you pass often, a ribbon on the sink faucet, a special flowering plant). Each time you pass the reminder, take 2 seconds to remember your intention.

PSYCHOLOGY:

Every space evokes feeling. What does your main living area feel like? What do you *want* it to feel like?

Take inventory for a few days (to rule out the hangry or messy frustration moments that can throw off analyses) and choose one thing you can do to make your living area feel more like your dream. Here are some ideas:

CALM: bring in a plant

INVITING: throw a blanket over a couch, include a foot rest, build a fire

FORMAL: carefully place pillows symmetrically

ENERGETIC: add a pop of the same color to three different places

PERSONAL: family pictures or a custom piece of art that sparks conversation

DESIGN TIP:

A great design secret is the rule known as the Golden Proportion, which is "⅔". When designing or decorating a space, try splitting the area into thirds, and arrange items so that the focus hits right at the ⅔ mark...a little more than half way, but still balanced.

Using the Golden Proportion adds interest and focus. Places where the Golden Proportion is especially helpful is hanging art (try placing artwork ⅓ of the way down from the ceiling), decorating fireplace mantels (instead of being exactly symmetrical, make the focal point a little off to one side and balance with less prominent decor on each side), and when placing pillows (try putting two pillows on one side of a couch, and one on the other).

INTERACT:

We all have tons of stuff to do.

It's part of daily survival.

You can't escape it.

Choose to take those to-do's on your list and use them as inspiration to connect with someone. Instead of just dropping off the dry cleaning, why not call a niece on the way and make that errand time "connection time"? Instead of weeding, make a fun game with prizes that go to each family member for unique contributions (i.e., "Pulled weed that looks the most like Dad" or "Best Dressed in the Garden" or "Bug Veterinarian")

By using our daily chores as opportunities, we own our roles as creators of the amount of joy we claim each day.

COZY UP:

What makes you really happy? Is it chocolate? (Are you human?) Is it the early morning sunshine? Is it a good book in a cozy chair? Make space in your house and home to experience the things you love on a daily basis!!

RESEARCH:

Researchers Evans and Cohen explored a theory known as "optimal stimulation". It may seem like common sense, but it's been shown that people respond negatively when both under- or over- stimulated, but an optimal level of stimulation allows for people to more easily experience healthy growth, positive regard toward others, performance, and good health (Evans & Cohen, 1987).

Conduct a quick internal check: how do you feel about the chaos or activity level in your home? Is the commotion over the top? Are you bored out of your mind? Choose one thing that you can do to help stimulation levels even out.

SEASONS OF LOVE:

Winter doesn't mean that romance has to be frozen too. On the contrary!!!! Make a date of it, and find (or make yourself) some really great hot chocolate and drink it wrapped in a blanket on your sofa or porch. Light a candle for even more magic.

ENTERTAIN:

Do you love having people over? Do you hate it? Either way, how can your make your house work FOR YOU in this regard? Look into finding an easily assemble-able, makes-your-heart-happy tray or set of cups that can be busted out at a moment's notice! maybe you hate that company can see a messy kitchen so you avoid inviting people in-- make your porch or entry really inviting so that you can have comfortable and connecting conversations right at the door. Or even better, leave dishes in the sink and invite people over on purpose just to stretch yourself.

FEBRUARY

CROSSROADS:

We often forget to schedule ourselves some transition time. It takes a minute to get settled when you get home (or husbands get home). It takes a minute (or 10, or 55) to get shoes on and children herded out the door. Plan for these comings and goings and in-between moments and give yourself some cushion, and therefore a little more patience and kindness and sanity.

HOLIDAY ADVANTAGE:

Valentine's Day is around the corner! Involve your kids and deck out your house with easy, inexpensive paper hearts and crepe paper. If you want, you could have the entire fam write/draw things and people they love on the hearts. I love paper decorations because they provide a connection moment to create, and if they get "loved" on by the younger ones, no one is out mucho dinero.

Word of warning: be intentional with your use of glitter, because although sparkly and exciting, it is magnetically attracted to all things and will never ever evvveeeerrr go away.

GET PICKY:

A tough aspect of design is whittling down (or accumulating) possessions so that what fills your home is both functional and, as Marie Kondo would say, "sparks joy." If you don't love a piece, it doesn't belong in your house.

Being well made ("They just don't make things like they used to!"), being enviable ("I know there are people that would kill to have this sofa."), feeling obligation ("But this vase was in my mother's house"), or having come from somewhere far away ("I can't get rid of this dead-ugly ratty chair because it's from Belguim") are NOT GOOD ENOUGH REASONS to buy or keep furniture, or anything for that matter. In our house, I have to "like it a level 9/10" to bring it in.

Sometimes things are largely functional (like an under-rug pad), but if I don't appreciate its functionality a 9/10, I can find a better item that I like more.

Maybe liking it is just as simple as liking not having spent a fortune on an item, but unless it was THAT good of a deal, and unless my heart sings sonnets, I'll keep looking. Consider donating the items that have served you to a new home where they will be appreciated anew.

The home should be the treasure chest of living.

- Le Corbusier

PERSPECTIVE:

Crawl around with your kids today- see the world at their level. It might surprise you how you feel or act! The perspective is enlightening.

CHILL:

Take five quiet minutes to sit still and do nothing but sip your favorite beverage.

DESIGN TIP:

When making a bed to look hotel-esque (or better), use two sleeping pillows, two big shams (I love Euro size), and 1-3 additional throw pillows for pops of color and texture.

Don't be afraid to mix patterns either. For this, think in terms of small, medium, and large, and get a balanced proportion of each. For example, get a small pattern sheet like a pinstripe, two medium pattern throw pillows like a buffalo plaid, and a large pattern throw pillow like an abstract floral in a similar color palette.

ELEVATE:

Find a stool that your toddler can use in the kitchen to help out with washing dishes, sorting vegetables, whacking spoons on all the forbidden things.

Getting kids involved early alongside you will instill a love for work, food, and communicating with you! Try searching the web for "IKEA hacks" to get your mind going.

RESEARCH:

The theory of affordances says that environments can suggest we behave a certain way (it "affords" behaviors). For example, a waiting room with chairs suggests that you sit. Or, an entryway with a shoe rack and bench invites you to remove your shoes upon entering (Gibson, 1977).

Similarly, what we decorate our homes with affects how our families think, feel, and behave. What are your furnishings, accessories, and pictures saying about and to those who live there? What are the "subliminal invitations" being offered?

INSPIRATION:

· ·

Whatever good things we build end up building us.

- Jim Rohn

· ·

We shape our buildings, and afterwards they shape us.

- Winston Churchill

· ·

APPRECIATE:

When you crawl into bed tonight take a minute to feel your blankets and sheets against you.

Do you like how they feel?

Are they silky? Soft? Fuzzy? Scratchy?

We spend a lot of our lives asleep in bed. Take the time and effort to make yours a sanctuary by choosing and loving your bedsheets.

MARCH

THE MADNESS:

March Madness is upon us!!! It might be easy to be annoyed with the excess basketball hooplah happening around the country (and in our own homes), but this March, get into it if someone you love is into it! Create a bracket! Make a treat! Watch a game! Pick a favorite player! Use this opportunity to connect with a loved one and show them that you value them, and their interests. If the interested one is you (my mom was always the sports watcher at our house), dive in and invite people to participate in your excitement!

ROUTINE AWARENESS:

Is there a place set apart in your home for personal private time? Everyone needs privacy, including your children. Jot down some ideas for personal spaces for you and those you live with.

CREATE:

Ask your children and/or spouse to tell you what their dream vacation would be. Keep a list of their answers (maybe write after the discussion) and see if you can repeat some of the common favorite elements in your next getaway.

.

CELEBRATE:

Sometimes the best celebrations are those that are completely elective. Choose something crazy, fun, or special that you can do with St. Patrick's Day that goes above and beyond the "oh dang, am I wearing green?" schtick. Here are some ideas to get your green juices flowing: color your milk green, hide chocolate gold coins throughout your house, eat Lucky Charms, watch that old Disney Channel classic "Luck of the Irish", hunt for four leaved clovers, wear everything green you own, let the kids paint your face festively, eat all sorts of green foods for dinner (lime jell-o, salad, green smoothies, green eggs and ham, etc.). Do something all-out and spontaneous, and don't tell a soul. Not on Instagram, nothing. Do it for the people you live with and those you will physically see throughout the day, and that's it.

DESIGN:

I get cranky when mud is tracked into my house. Choose something frustrating that happens in your house and then figure out a solution. I'm going to get a really sturdy rug for my back door. One that makes me jubilant. Now join with me in swearing off discouragement when the solution fails a few times, and instead, embracing the messiness and unpredictability of life with people we love!

MAKE A MESS:

Houses get messy. And that's the point. Make an intentional mess today with your family and have a lot of fun doing it. Make the memory worth the mess! When I was elementary school aged, my dad mopped the floor squeaky clean, cleared the furniture from the kitchen, and was sitting in his swimming suit with my baby brother in the middle of the floor when I got home from school. Next to him was a gallon-sized can of chocolate pudding. Once my brothers got home too, we changed into our own swimming suits and skated through pudding all afternoon. It was awesome. And SO MESSY. Afterward, Dad paid us a quarter for every spot of pudding we could find. It just so happens that Mom was out of town that day, and she didn't know about our escapades until weeks later.

RELAX:

Society tells us we need to look a certain way ourselves and that our homes need to also look a certain way. THROW IT OUT THE WINDOW. Not your stuff. Just the pressure. Today, look how you are, and live how you are, and embrace it. Stop "should-ing" yourself. Just be you today. Feel the love!!

RESEARCH:

Urie Bronfenbrenner (1979). studied the influence of context on development and interaction. His whole theory (ecological systems theory) says that the closest context we operate within is our families, our homes, our peers, our schools, and the immediate places and social systems we directly encounter. These have huge impacts on how we live, think, and behave.

The next layer, or system, of influence is the interaction of the first layer elements (how mom feels about teacher, dad about the house, etc).

There are five systems all together, each getting a little more removed from the individual. The most interesting part of ecological systems theory to me is that we are influenced by so many forces, people, and energies, and we influence so much as well. What influence are you making? What impact is your home having on your relationships, personal well-being, and the health of those closest to you?

INSPIRATION FROM A MASTER:

. . . .

Concision in style, precision in thought, decision in life.

– Victor Hugo

. . . .

IT'S IN THE AIR:

Springtime brings some awesome holidays!! Think over your Easter, April Fools', Passover, and other spring traditions and decide what is enjoyable and meaningful for your family.

My family always takes our decorated Easter eggs to a huge hill in town where we proceed to roll them all down the hill until the break into a gazillion pieces for the seagulls to feast upon later. There are races and protection plans and usually some long distance records. I didn't realize this was unusual until I got married, and now I love it all the more.

APRIL

APPRECIATION OF THE SEASON:

Spring is in bloom!! Take some time this month to adventure around your home, yard, and neighborhood to smell the roses, appreciate the budding and blooming trees, and soak in some sunshine!!

ROUTINE:

Hang up a growth chart somewhere in your home and take everyone's measurements. Try to record the changes a couple of times a year! It might be fun to also include a one word description of the kids' current likes/loves/obsessions/funny things.

Today, I'd write next to my son "Lightening McQueen." I guess that's two words. But a whole slew of cartoon loving memories are certainly embodied in that image... potty training with McQueen underwear (hallelujah), playing with Mater toys all day long, and yelling "KACHOW!" whenever jumping. Another son would receive the "eyebrows" tag- his little brows are the most emotionally descriptive things I've ever seen. Hilarious.

FAMILY:

Kids learn a TON from working alongside parents. There's something pretty amazing that happens when hands are busy.... usually mouths and hearts open. Choose a chore you usually delegate or knock out alone, and include a child to do it WITH you. Do the task not to just get it done, but to connect with, teach, and enjoy your child. Take deep breaths when the toilet brush becomes a magic wand and when the vacuum cord becomes Spiderman webs.

SAFETY:

Childproofing (read: destructive/curious toddler-proofing) a home is no simple task, yet it's a necessary one given how quick those little squirts can get into mischief. My favorite child proofing find has been magnetic closures on our kitchen cupboards. Each time we need to open the cupboard we have to use the magnetic "key", but I feel like my kids are safe and can roam our home freely. That's a piece of sanity that is priceless.

DESIGN:

When choosing colors for a room, choose neutrals for the expensive and hard-to-change elements (sofas, bedroom furniture), and get fun and creative with those things that are easily updated (rugs, throws, even paint if you're daring).

AWARENESS:

Part of life and love is protecting our homes and our families. Take a minute to consider how much you know about your children's friends and their families. If you'd like to know more, make an effort to connect with the friend and the family-- often life-long family relationships are made this way.

RELAX:

Today you have permission to do nothing productive. Go with the flow and see where it takes you.

I'm serious.

Don't even shower unless it sounds absolutely thrilling.

RESEARCH:

Abraham Maslow. A man with some serious genius. He brought us the "hierarchy of needs," which helps us identify where to start when we feel all out of sorts (1970). His hierarchy is in pyramid shape, with the foundational elements being at the bottom and with each layer building upon the last until the peak. The layers, from bottom to top, are as follows: Physiological (food, water, shelter, love), Safety (emotional and physical security), Love/Belonging (relationships), Esteem (confidence, respect), and Self-Actualization (creativity, spontaneity, problem solving). Where are you operating most of the time?

FRESHEN UP:

Get some fresh flowers or greenery for your home today. Nature does miracles for mood.

INSPIRATIONAL QUOTE:

Simplicity is the ultimate sophistication.

- Leonardo Da Vinci

MAY

CELEBRATE:

This month brings Cinco de Mayo!! Prep for today by making a quick stop by the dollar store for a piñata and paper plates, then party with great food like chips and salsa (or 7 layer dip!!), tacos, and frozen limeaides!!

Additionally, it is necessary to note that the 4th is Star Wars Day. Everyone should celebrate Star Wars Day. May the Fourth be with you.

I LIKE TO MOVE IT:

Sometimes we think that we have to "exercise" to lead a healthy lifestyle. Today, instead of worrying about counting steps or getting 20 minutes of cardio, do something active around your home, such as gardening, vacuuming, dancing, cleaning, carrying laundry upstairs, scrubbing baseboards, mowing the lawn, or emptying all of the trash cans. Move because you have a body and do something you love!

FAMILY:

Take a picture of yourself with your kids. Replace any and all negative thoughts about yourself or your body with positive ones. Moms are the best. Let yourself relax about executing the perfect duck-face selfie and capture some fun with your children, who grow all too quickly.

CREATE:

Approach your home with curiosity today. Instead of feeling the pull of anxiety and urgency to get things done, consider what you'd like to see happen and see if you can find a way to make it happen filled with hope, wonder, and growth-mindedness.

DESIGN TIP:

When considering a new home, take into account the view into your home from the front door. Sometimes it's nice to have the option of keeping projects or toys or dishes out of view initially, then if you want, you can invite people into the real life, living and breathing home experience. (But not every salesman or quick chat needs that invitation by default.)

Also consider the view *out* the front door, and be intentional about what you want to see first when you leave your home every day.

COME IN:

One of the many valuable things we can do with our homes
is extend a warm welcome to family members and friends.
Here are a few ideas to setting the stage of welcome to all who
enter your home: make a sign that specifically can address
each returning (or visiting) party ("Welcome, Jensens! We're
happy you're here!"), play inviting music, light a candle for
ambience and a tasty smell, bake cookies so that the smell can
be eaten too!, put a pretty plant on the front porch, get a
custom welcome mat, take a minute to put down your task at
hand to personally greet each person as they walk through the
door.

RELAX:

Let the kids do things as slowly as they'd like today. Try to enjoy the process.

RESEARCH:

Architectural depth is a principle that describes the way homes get more private and intimate the deeper you progress into them (Hillier & Hanson, 1984).

For instance, a front yard is very open to the public, especially if no architectural barriers have been crossed to enter (such as a fence). A front door offers the first architectural symbol of intimacy, and from there, hallways, turns, and more doors symbolize the filtration that homes provide for safety, privacy, and belonging. Knowing this helps us set up our homes to feel appropriately open or private, depending on what we wish.

INSPIRATION:

As your build, clean, care for, and decorate your home, remember that homes are physical symbols of spiritual components. Make your home represent physically what you feel about home spiritually.

. . . .

Imagine yourself as a living house. God comes in to rebuild that house. At first, perhaps, you can understand what He is doing. He is getting the drains right and stopping the leaks in the roof and so on; you knew that those jobs needed doing and so you are not surprised. But presently He starts knocking the house about in a way that hurts abominably and does not seem to make any sense. What on earth is He up to? The explanation is that He is building quite a different house from the one you thought of - throwing out a new wing here, putting on an extra floor there, running up towers, making courtyards. You thought you were being made into a decent little cottage: but He is building a palace. He intends to come and live in it Himself.

- C.S. Lewis

. . . .

MORE INSPIRATION:

. . . .

Think more, design less.

- Ellen Lupton

. . . .

JUNE

JUNE BLISS:

It's summer!!!!! My awesome neighbor has successfully raised her family into adulthood, and one day while we were chatting, she told me of one of their favorite family summer traditions that I love. She would freeze fruit juice and smoothie leftovers in ice trays (there's always little remnants left over, right?), cut up a watermelon, and fill a big bowl with it all (watermelon, juice popsicles, and some regular old ice too) and put it on the porch. Her kids were occupied, fed, and happy for hours. That's dreamy, right?

FIND YOUR ZEN ZONE:

Are you being intentional about the sleep you're getting? Whether it's 4 hours or 10, do you know what YOUR body needs to function optimally? Try experimenting with sleep and see if you can hone in on your individual preferences and needs.

FAMILY:

REcreate in summer: live a childhood memory with your kids.

SHOW ME THOSE PEARLY WHITES:

Smile today. Be a happy wife and a fun mom. Not fun in the crazy sense, but fun in the "enjoys life and can make any moment positive" kind of way.

DESIGN:

When we think of our homes it's easy to address what we need and want and like RIGHT NOW. Get out a biiiiigg piece of paper and outline what life will look like for your family as you progress through different life stages. Start by setting up a 2, 5, 10, 20 year plan. It might look like this: In 2 years, Jonny will be 6, Eliza will be 10, and Josh will be 13. They'll probably be just about through with our playroom. Maybe we can start to think of how we'll use that room when they get to this age.

USE IT!:

Creativity loves constraints. Don't be afraid to embrace your unique circumstances, life stage, preferences, values, and current space. Get creative!

RELAX:

When you find your buffers have left and you're getting easily upset/frustrated, take a minute to do a personal inventory: Have you eaten? Are you distracted? Are your feelings hurt? Address the root cause of your discomfort and acknowledge the feeling of annoyance as a warning sign that something is off. Take a few deep breaths for all the many reasons, and reconnect with your strength and your vision of who you want to be. Then go get 'em!

RESEARCH:

We are a sanitizing, sterilizing, 5-second-rule abandoning nation of people, and it might be affecting our health negatively. Recently, researchers found that anti-bacterial soap wasn't all that effective, and the anti-bacterial soap was banned all together! (Interestingly, this same ingredient is present in our toothpaste and other household items.) We need the goodness that is contained in dirt. We need the probiotics in soil. We need to let our personal microbiomes flourish. One way to do this is to get our hands in dirt often. Another way is to skip the sanitizer and opt for regular old, effective and safe soap and water. And if you're feeling particularly ambitious, try showering a little less often.

INSPIRE:

One of my heroes, Marjorie Pay Hinckley, once said, "I don't want to drive up to the pearly gates in a shiny sports car, wearing beautifully, tailored clothes, my hair expertly coiffed, and with long, perfectly manicured fingernails. I want to drive up in a station wagon that has mud on the wheels from taking kids to scout camp. I want to be there with a smudge of peanut butter on my shirt from making sandwiches for a sick neighbors children. I want to be there with a little dirt under my fingernails from helping to weed someone's garden. I want to be there with children's sticky kisses on my cheeks and the tears of a friend on my shoulder. I want the Lord to know I was really here and that I really lived."

While making messes, we make memories. Consider making more messes this month and let those messes show that we really lived.

EASY AS 1-2-3:

Designate a thrilling "Pick A Letter Day" Celebration! Choose any letter you'd like, and try to do as many things as possible that day that start with your celebratory letter. Eat toast and tacos, go to the theater, taste test taffy, twirl, twist-tie stuff closed, tour a museum, try out a Tesla, tailgate, throw tomahawks, wear tiaras... really the possibilities are endless.

JULY

REMEMBER:

Since I'm American, July to me means celebrating patriotism and heritage. Tell your kids a few fun stories about the founding fathers and a couple of your own ancestors! Show pictures and invite the kids to memorize names (or even nicknames!) so that the lessons from the stories become part of their real lives.

PARTY:

Play a board or yard game with the family! Our favorites are bocce ball, freeze tag, bike obstacle course, dice games, Old Maid, Slap Jack, Rook, Phase 10, Trouble, and frisbee.

SLOW IT DOWN:

Lay in the grass and look at the clouds passing. Try this alone, or include your sweetheart and/or littles!

GREENIFY:

The benefits of cleaning with natural ingredients are so fun to think about! I love that my toddlers can play under my sink and the only risk is a mess. I love that when my 5 year old spills laundry soap I'm not worried he'll break out in a rash. I love that if my kids get too much toothpaste I don't have to call poison control. Become aware of the startling, scientific, and real power of vinegar and consider reaping the benefits of a "naturally cleaned" home.

DESIGN:

Our family tradition is to head to the mountains for the Fourth of July. We all stay at a popular ski destination and enjoy all the summer festivities (hiking, parades, parks, tennis, golf, sitting around together, playing games, swimming). My grandmother was (and her legacy still reigns) reliable in her decoration of her hotel room. There were flags in plants and USA bears on couches and red, white, and blue M&M's on the coffee table. I'm pretty sure she found a way to hang a wreath on the door too. Of the hotel. It was a little over-kill but, hey. While I'm not suggesting everyone should bring a bin of decorations for every vacation, I do believe in the power of a few props to "set the stage" for a celebration. Engage the sense of sight the next time you want to communicate the importance of an event, person, or ritual.

ENTERTAIN:

Don't apologize for anything when company comes over this month. Just love your guests.

RELAX:

Every time you pass a mirror this month, strike a pose (especially in front of the kids!) and exclaim "What a hottie!!!" Invite the kids to join in, and tell them each one thing you like about them every time you pass the mirror ("Boy, you sure have sparkling eyes!" "I can't even believe how tall you are!" "What a strong body you have!" "I love how the color red looks with your shiny hair.")

RESEARCH:

The home environment has the potential to interact with human temperament to trigger specific behaviors. Especially for children with sensory reactivity tendencies or heightened novelty awareness, overstimulation can be a real thing. Calmness or aggression can be triggered for children depending on texture, lighting, sound, and social pressure. Take an intentional look at the home you live in, and consider if any of your family members experience sensory overload based on the way they input information (Evans, Nelson, & Porter, 2012).

PICTURE THIS:

The key to making an awesome gallery wall is using things that you love. Keep an eye out for objects of all shapes and sizes, and do your best to only use things that mean something to you. I love pictures, both paintings and photographs, and think that multiple visual representations of "who our family is" is very important. Use pictures from your phones, from a professional session, or draw them yourself, but make your house walls sing "You belong here! I belong here! This is us."

—Top 5 Ideas for A Cool and Personal Gallery Wall--

1- Use items and images that are personally meaningful.

2- Mix up candid and formal photography.

3- Include different mediums beyond just frames of pictures, such as wooden letters, shelving, clocks, mirrors, etc, to create an eclectic look. For a more formal feel, buy matching frames and choose photos that have the same coloring and feel, such as "black and white candids".

4- Plan out your gallery wall on the floor in front of the wall. Use the golden proportion to help you decide where the centerline of the picture mass (official title) should end up. Get someone to help you so that you can have perspective on the whole wall and someone to help you when hanging things. The best way I've found to decide where a nail goes is to hold the picture up where you want it, put your finger behind the picture on the spot designated for a nail (either on the string-- be sure to pull it up to make it taut, or on the bracket), slide your finger the micro-inches onto the corresponding place on the wall, have your gallery-wall-making-bestie grab the picture and hand you a hammer while you replace your finger with a nail, and hammer that nail in.

5- Recognize that walls are typically very easily repairable, and you can take calculated risks in hanging stuff. I know some people who go years without decorating their homes because they don't want to "mess up the walls". Yes, you don't want to make huge, unnecessary holes, but what great real estate to infuse your home with meaning and inspiration. Don't let the fear of making a mess keep you from making a home. Put that on a pillow. Or in your gallery wall.

PRIORITIZE:

We typically tend to have too much stuff. We accumulate for a variety of reasons, but when it comes down to it, we spend a lot of time worrying about caring for, cleaning, protecting, hanging, packing the stuff we don't even use. Be honest and get rid of that stuff that no longer suits you! Do a purge about every 6 months, and become the boss of your stuff, not the other way around. Only let the favorite, most dear, most functional things stick around.

AUGUST

· ·

TRADITIONS:

When my husband and I were newlywed college kids, we started an August tradition of living as simply and carefully as we possibly could with regard to finances in order to make the last sprint of tuition saving for the fall semester. We didn't go out to eat, we didn't have expensive date nights, we didn't buy new clothes or give elaborate gifts. We even tried to avoid the grocery store! Okay, we were a little desperate. We called it "Amish August" because we wanted to embody the simplicity and care that is characteristic of the Amish people in order to cash flow our education. It was fun to take a few weeks and see what we could really do without. Surprisingly, we did just fine with much less than we expected. We've tried to continue this tradition ever since!

THE GOODS:

Peaches are ripening!!!! Do some research about a neighborhood farm or orchard and go visit as a family. Lots of farms will let you come pick your own produce! I love peaches just by themselves, but we also love making peach milkshakes, peach oatmeal, and "peach bowls" with yogurt and granola. I can't even talk about my cousin's peach pie without shedding tears of joy. Don't let seasonal produce pass you by!

FAMILY:

. . . .

Never let a problem to be solved become more important than a person to be loved.

- Thomas Monson

. . . .

BREATHE DEEPLY:

Indoor air quality can be easily worse for our health than outdoor air quality. From the buildings to the carpets to the recirculation, we could use some freshening up around our homes! House plants are an awesome way to filter your indoor air.

Consider adding a new addition (or 5!) to your home! Plants are relatively inexpensive and there are certain plants that are low-maintenance as well. In addition, caring for plants can be an opportunity for family members to claim responsibility over something other than themselves, which encourages health also (Jones, 1999).

DESIGN:

August is the month of summer appreciation, I think. We notice that fall is fast approaching and we want to soak in every last ray of summer goodness before it escapes again. One of my favorite summer-soaking-rituals is sitting on the porch in the evening. Sometimes weeding if I'm feeling it. Consider making a space to appreciate the seasons from your home, whether it be a chair on the porch, a window that can be opened or romantically gazed from, or maybe even seasonal plants or bird feeders.

READY, BREAK!:

Take a break from all forms of media today: TV, social media, radio. Instead, together as a family write notes, letters, or color pictures for someone special and mail it. Get out your blankets and build a fort. Make a family band from misc kitchen objects. As we put down our screens and the noise of never-ending-updates, we can connect more easily with the people around us.

RELAX:

Only allow a To-Do List of 4 items today! Scary? Absolutely. But relish the simplicity, and only choose the four most important things you could possibly do today. Consider the absolute worst case scenario... what if the dishes DON'T GET DONE today?!?!

REMEMBER:

Anxiety and depression are becoming a common struggle. While everyone experiences blue moods and worry, chronic depression and anxiety can be truly life-hindering. If you or someone you love is among these, brainstorm what you can do to fill your life, your home, and your heart with the love of God. Fear is often a root of anxiety and depression. The best anecdote I've found for fear is faith, and the hardest part of faith for me is simply remembering:

Remembering that I'm loved.
Remembering that all things will work out for good.
Remembering that I am enough and my efforts are adequate.
Remembering that I will be led.
Remembering that as I seek, I will find.

Consider reminding yourself of the truths you know by creating focal points in your home that either symbolically or literally represent what you want to remember. This can be done with flowers, typography, art of all kinds, even furniture.

CELEBRATE:

School is on the horizon. Consider starting a tradition to commemorate the occasion! Some ideas might include a School-Eve Dinner or gift each child a "lucky pencil" infused with your love and faith in them for the new school year.

ENJOY:

Turn on the sprinklers and let the kids go at it!

JOIN IN!

I know, getting your hair wet means like 30 minutes of extra work. Do it!

SEPTEMBER

SEASON APPRECIATION:

Carve apples this month, and bake them so they resemble tasty shrunken heads! If you want, seek out local apple orchards and make a day of picking, cleaning, and eating the fall's most tasty fruit!

YOU FIRST:

When you find yourself frustrated with something another person is doing, or if you want to see a change happen in your family or work arenas, start with yourself.

YOU start learning math a little better, and show your teen that math is fun and important.

YOU put your clothes right away when you take them off, respecting your property and the feel of the home.

YOU eat your vegetables, because you want to be strong and healthy.

YOU turn down the volume of your favorite show, because others are doing other things close by.

YOU look people in the eyes when you talk to them, because it shows respect and attention.

As you start to do the things you say you value, others will notice your cheer and enthusiasm and want to do it with you. It's basically magic.

FAMILY:

Invite the kids to help with dinner more often this month. Make it easier for them to be at the counter by building or buying stools specifically designed for kids at counters. If the kids are too young to chop, stir, or peel, have them sit at the counter and separate a big bowl of beans (white from black). The key here is to get their hands busy and interacting with you while you tackle a task.

BEAUTIFY:

Learn how to fold clothes, towels, and sheets really beautifully. After I did this, laundry folding became WAY more fun! My drawers and linen closets also look a lot better too! Search YouTube for a variety of methods and tips. I have found the Konmari method to be my personal choice.

DESIGN TIP:

When arranging furniture, try to envision "connection opportunity". Make little intentional opportunities for reading together, having meaningful conversations, and playing tag. We sometimes get stuck in the rut of pushing all of our furniture against the walls, but if you leave a foot or two between the wall and furniture, it creates the feeling of space and intimacy, and also makes a great hiding spot for hide-and-seek. Don't be afraid to use the center of the room for things either, and if it helps, think of the grouping as a rock in the middle of the lava that is necessary for survival if you're ever going to get "across" safely.

The takeaway point is this: space is a tool. Use it, all of it, and love the people in your life.

SCREEN LOVE:

TV has a bad rap. Kind of deserves it in most cases. However, TV can be used for great things too. Today and this week, try to be really aware of when and what you are watching. Consider intentionally choosing to watch your 1-3 top shows and eliminating the surfing. Another idea is to find something to pair with TV watching occasionally: cuddling with a loved one, folding laundry, exercising, cleaning.

RELAX:

Mop the floor with some old socks on your feet and some great tunes turned way up.

RESEARCH:

Erik Erikson (1968) is famous for identifying eight stages of psychosocial development that happen in order from infancy through adulthood. Each stage is also associated with a guiding virtue. Being aware of these stages is helpful because sometimes it's hard to know what is age appropriate for our children (and ourselves!!) to be working through. This month, be intentional about connecting with your peers, parents, siblings, children, and grandchildren the virtues associated with their stage of development, and be flexible as they, and you, make mistakes in learning.

AGE	LESSON	VIRTUE
0-1.5	Trust vs. Mistrust	Hope
1.5-3	Autonomy vs. Shame	Will
3-5	Initiative vs. Guilt	Purpose
5-12	Industry vs. Inferiority	Competency
12-18	Identity vs. Role Confusion	Fidelity
18-40	Intimacy vs. Isolation	Love
40-65	Generativity vs. Stagnation	Care
65+	Ego Integrity vs. Despair	Wisdom

CHARM:

Character is the feeling of depth and story that a home provides. While some homes may be brand new, the character shines through a space by the way meaningful items are utilized and the personal elements that are included within. Here are three steps to boosting the character element of your home:

1- Incorporate history into your decor, even if your home is a more streamlined, modern aesthetic. You could frame old familial photographs, use sturdy or unique wood in the construction of your furniture, or use interesting or antique door knobs or mirrors.

2- Create an accent wall with an interesting material or pattern.

3- Bring in texture with blankets or pillows.

CHALLENGE:

Only take five minutes to do your hair and makeup once a week this month. Set the timer! Use the time you save to connect with someone you love.

OCTOBER

APPRECIATE:

October is a time of harvest and gratitude, though often we wait until November to traditionally celebrate these things. Appreciate your friendships and the important people in your life by inviting one or two families over for a low key breakfast-for-dinner night, or a leftover potluck. Try to let the relationship shine through as being the reason for the gathering, and let the food and "proper hosting techniques" fall aside just for one night.

TRUST:

Find a way to let the toddler "do it all by himself" this month. Oi Vay!

FAMILY:

Sometimes I dread the fall time because of the ever-present football season. I do love football, but occasionally I feel threatened by it! This month, make an awesome treat for the big game (or even a smaller one) and sit down with your husband (and kids too!) to enjoy the season and tradition of it all as a family. We all love to feel that our hobbies and interests are supported! If football isn't a thing for your family, find another way to support your husband in his passions and interests.

PROTECT:

Put together a "monster spray" (or something similar) of water and a few drops of yummy smelling essential oils. Maybe add a little glitter too! Whenever anyone feels scared, spritz the spray on them and all around, and remind them that they are safe and loved.

DESIGN:

Design involves taking risks. What's something you would LOVE to do with your home that just scares you? Paint a wall? Put up some wallpaper? Actually hammer some nails into the walls? DO IT! Get the crazy couch you can't stop thinking about. Hang a unique light fixture. Dedicate a corner somewhere to your wild sewing projects. Make your home design fun and exciting, and take a few risks. My caution is that risks can be expensive, so start small if you need to, and don't go into debt. Calculated risks, however, are a huge win.

ENTERTAIN:

Use in-season, natural decor as a centerpiece! This month, find a few new uses for pumpkins!

RELAX:

Have a family art gallery night. Everyone can create a piece or two and display it on the wall, and on the big night, dress up, serve "fancy" appetizers, and walk around talking about the hidden symbolism or rich meaning of everyone's pieces.

RESEARCH:

One of my favorite marriage specialists is Bill Doherty. On his website, SmartMarriages.com, he talks about the importance of intentional marriage and gives some examples of how to create meaningful rituals as a couple. One that particularly sticks out to me is a scenario called "Top the Dog!", in which a couple tries to be more excited than the dog is when their partner comes home. This month, be intentional about how you show your spouse appreciation.

UPGRADE:

Social media is so helpful and fun while also annoying, addicting, and cluttering of the mind/spirit. Is social media good? Bad? The truth is that it's neither. How social media works for YOU is a completely unique situation to play with. This month, be aware of how you are engaging with your social media technology, and perhaps try to filter out the unnecessary in favor of more uplifting, inspiring, or refreshing content/activities.

INFUSE:

Read something interesting and discuss it at dinner with your family, or laminate a few maps and use them as placemats! Use dinner time to be a place of learning, connecting, and dreaming. How is your dining room set up? Research heralds regular family dinner as being one of the most influential routines in a child's life, leading to academic success and emotional resilience. Make sure your space is adequate and inviting to make that happen for your family.

NOVEMBER

SEASONAL APPRECIATION:

How cozy is November?!? This month, feel the coziness by watching a fire. That's right-- light a candle, build a fire in the fireplace, or make a fire (contained and safe, right?) outside. Take time to watch the flames and let yourself appreciate the warmth of the moment.

HEAR IT:

Take a minute to listen to Tim McGraw's rendition of "Humble and Kind". Isn't the message grand?

Seek music that uplifts you personally and shares positive messages. Music has an amazing ability to set the tone for any experience-- have you ever had to cover your ears during a scary movie to get your heart rate under control, or has a song triggered the memory of a specific event? Be intentional about the tunes that make up the soundtrack for your life.

FAMILY:

Recently, the principle of returning and reporting has been reinforced to me. When we follow up with others on the tasks and experiences we have stewardship over, we create the opportunity to receive feedback, strengthen relational connection, and feel encouragement. Consider requiring your children to check in with you often so that you can experience these benefits with them also!

VISUALIZE:

Identify a peaceful person that you admire. Why do you admire him or her? What is his approach to everyday tasks? How does she make you feel? What can you learn and apply from the way he prepares for and executes the big and little things in his life? What about this person can you incorporate into your daily lifestyle?

DESIGN:

Pillows are like t-shirts. You want to be able to feel comfortable with them. They need to be versatile and sturdy. They need to look good at a moment's notice. They need to pull a room together without breaking the bank. And they need to stand up to the wear and tear of family life: throwing, sleeping on, squishing, tossing, fluffing, and even washing. When shopping for throw pillows, shake them around a bit!! Pull gently to check for use-ability issues. If it molts, don't even put it in the cart. If it lumps, stretches, slumps, or squishes strangely, it's not worth it. See how the pillow reforms after a few good whacks, sitting on it, shaking it, and throwing it at unsuspecting customers. JOKING. Just joking. Come on, we're classy around here.

TAKE IT HIGHER:

The comparison trap is a real thing!! We can see what other people are doing ALL THE TIME. Often the things we see are artistic renditions of life that we interpret as goals for reality. How can we engage with others without falling into the pitfalls of comparison? The answer is simple but difficult: get centered in who YOU are. Dig in deep and remember you worth, your mission, and your contributions, then don't forget them. When we are centered ourselves, we can love others without feeling attacked.

RELAX:

Wear a perfume that makes you happy. If possible, try to find a scent that is made from natural ingredients, perhaps an essential oil. Lovely plus non-toxic is always a bonus.

INSPIRE:

. . . .

Content precedes design. Design in the absence of content is not design, it's decoration.

- Jeffrey Zeldman

. . . .

GRATITUDE:

'Tis the season of thanksgiving! Let your heart and your mind fill with appreciation for all the bounty you enjoy. Be grateful for the good things, and even strive to be grateful for the less-than-good things, because sometimes those hiccups and trials are where our lives become sacred and our experiences become memorable.

DARE:

Helen Keller is quoted as saying that "Life is either a daring adventure or nothing at all." It's one of my favorite quotes of all time actually. Even quiet and personal matters can be seen as great adventures of growth and courage. This month, try to see the stress of the holidays as daring adventures. And feel free to nix anything that doesn't feel that way. If it stresses you out, bag it! Or at least find an adventurous approach.

DECEMBER

SERIOUS SEASONAL APPRECIATION:

The holiday season is a decidedly special time of year. Coming off of the gratitude high of Thanksgiving, we enter into the Christmas season with all of its splendor. I have a cousin that sends us a list of "December Family Fun" activities to sign up for and put on our calendars to make the holidays special. I love this tradition because participation is very low pressure- you just come when you can! We do all sorts of things, from concerts to sledding to stories and singing to brunch. It's fun to anticipate special, small things throughout the month with people we love that turn our spirits to celebrating the birth of Jesus Christ.

CINDERELLA LIFE LESSONS:

"Have courage, and be kind." Also, be careful about how many kernels of corn you stack under your chin…

WORTH IT:

Sometimes we have the tendency to "save the nice china" for "special occasions." We don't want to use the meaningful, beautiful, or expensive items daily for some reason, and instead keep things locked in cupboards or attics for the rare dinner party holiday (adults only, of course). I've historically been the worst with this... I have kept tags on clothes and purchases in boxes for a few weeks just to bask in their unadulterated newness! Luckily, I had a friend invite me to throw away all of my chipped, ugly, mismatched dish ware and replace it with something I loved and intended to use daily. I now use my nice bone china (a sleek, beautiful white variety) every day with three little boys (all under 5 years old). If they chip, I can replace them! Each time we eat with these dishes I am reminded that now is a special occasion, and these are the most important people in my life.

TEEN CONNECTION:

As a teenager, I got to know a wonderful woman who greeted her children coming home from weekend outings with a loaf of freshly baked bread. I thought this was amazing, of course. A few years later, she told me about her reasoning. She said that she knew she'd have ten minutes of debriefing time if she had something great to eat ready when her kids returned home. They would sit down, eat a piece or two of hot bread, and tell her all about what they were up to that night. Isn't that perfect? Use the food to love the people, that's what I say.

One of the kids who grew up with this fantastic tradition wrote this poem about her experience, and when I read it I'm so inspired to make my own "connection ritual" with my own kids:

Bread baking in the kitchen-
The steam rising in the air,
The first slice ready for the fixin'
Taken all day because she cares.

Coming home from school
The smell of bread before I even come inside.
Talking with my mother about how I was a feelin'
And eating with her side by side.

I love to talk and eat her bread,
It's a way she shows her love for me.
After eating and sharing my day with her
I feel like I've been fed,
Not only with her wisdom,
But also with her bread.

DESIGN:

Holiday decorating is SO FUN!!

It also can be a little overwhelming. The key to successful holiday decor is like anything else: balance. The first rule, of course, is to be calm and to make the act of decorating an intentional decision. Don't feel pressured or obligated to deck the halls. If you like holly and lights, put them up. If you'd really rather not, then don't. There are so many wonderful ways to celebrate a season, and decor is only one of them. However, if you become a crazy person, I can almost guarantee that no one is enjoying anything.

For a fun middle-of-the-path approach to making your home feel festive, try these quick but big-impact ideas:
1- Hang a wreath. (You can make, buy, thrift, or borrow!)

2- Burn a candle. Choose something that smells like the holidays to you and make it part of your family memories this year!

3- Put out a seasonal pillow or two.

4- Decorate your Christmas tree as a family (maybe just with lights!), and make it a tradition to watch the tree all lit up in the dark while playing music.

5- Make the mantle and tabletop focal points. My grandma decorated every inch of her house for Christmas right down to her toilet lids. This is 100% true. Festive music even played when you pulled on the toilet paper. She was basically a magician. While that is fun, the mantle and the tabletop are going to make a big difference for just a touch of work. Try candles, stockings, branches, fresh greenery, jars of ornaments, a nativity, or anything else you happen to love.

6- (Extra Credit) Swap out a familiar painting or print in your home for a character-filled depiction of some holiday element. We were given a framed vintage poster of Santa that comes out every December in our house. I love that the statement is big and my wall is refreshed. I also like that he goes away in January.

JUST DO IT:

Holiday season can get incredibly nutty and chaotic!! This month, do your best to not leave clutter-inducing to-do's hanging around. Your mind and your counter don't need any more to keep track of! When a bill comes in, pay it. When junk sweeps through the door in backpacks or in flyers, note what you need to on the calendar, make good decisions quickly, and get rid of the evidence. Find a place to display the Christmas cards that come in the mail that you can appreciate (and get those envelopes off the junk pile!). Taste the yummy goodies that neighbors drop by, have a moment of deep appreciation for the taste, texture, effort, and kindness that went into them, and then toss the remnants. Ain't nobody needin' to constantly snack on sugar (for at least 39 reasons). We need our charity and clarity out in full force this time of year, and brain fog and sugar crashes only add to the mayhem. Instead, choose something healthy and beautiful to take center stage on the counter that can satisfy a sweet tooth, a hungry belly, and a social pull, all without sabotaging our hearts and minds-- oranges perhaps?

RELAX:

Make yourself a sacred space, where you can breathe, reconnect with your higher self and Higher Power, and recenter. After you have your space, go there twice a day and whenever else you need a boost. Consider lighting a candle (or switching on an electric one), including a comfortable sitting area, and appreciating an essential oil you are crazy about. When we are full of love and light we are happier, and others are benefited by merely being around us. Let gratitude and love rule the day. Take time to remember.

RESEARCH:

Reminding ourselves that we belong makes us want to be where we are. A researcher named Irvin Altman and his colleague William Hansen found that college students were more likely to stay in school when they decorated their dorm rooms with scenes of them engaged in campus activities with school people and other rah-rah school paraphernalia. This works at home too! If you want to be more happy where you are, remind yourself of all the great things about your life by putting up pictures that make you say "OH that's amazing! (or beautiful, or sweet, or liberating)." Incorporate your travel souvenirs into your bookshelf decor. Put up a picture that reminds you to stop sweating the small stuff, perhaps of a person, ancestor, place, or event that truly inspires you (Hansen & Altman, 1975).

INSPIRE:

. . . .

It's through mistakes that you actually can grow. You have
to get bad in order to get good.

- Paula Scher

. . . .

ONWARD AND UPWARD:

There's always a time between setting a goal and achieving it. I'd wager that more than half of attaining any given goal is credited to seeing it, breathing it, visualizing it, and creating it spiritually. As we work toward our goals in every aspect of life with gratitude for the process (and the end goal itself, even if it hasn't quite materialized yet!) and a creation mindset, we can do anything. Being truly grateful, even if our dreams aren't yet realized, is the key to happiness and success.

CONCLUSION

Now that you've been an intentional witness to the seasons and the opportunities that each month holds, I hope that you'll take this book and create long lasting memories. I hope that you will adopt the things that worked for you and tweak the things that weren't quite right, and share with your friends and family the joy of seeing the sacred in the things commonly called "mundane."

God bless,

Carly

REFERENCES

Bronfenbrenner, U. (1979). *The ecology of human development: Experiments by nature and design.* Cambridge, MA: Harvard University Press.

Emmons, R. A., & McCullough, M. E. (2003). *Counting blessings versus burdens: an experimental investigation of gratitude and subjective well-being in daily life.* Journal of Personal and Social Psychology, 84, 344-377.

Erikson, E. H. (1968). Identity: Youth and crisis. New York: Norton.

Evans, G. W. & Cohen, S. (1987). Environmental stress. In D. Stokols & I. Altman, (Eds.), *Handbook of environmental psychology* (pp. 571-610). New York: John Wiley.

Evans, C. A., Nelson, J. L., & Porter C. L. (2012). Making Sense of Their World: Sensory Reactivity and Novelty Awareness as Aspects of Temperament and Correlates of Social Behaviours in Early Childhood. *Infant and Child Development, 21,* 503-520.

Gibson, J. J. (1977). The theory of affordances. In R. E. Shaw & J. Bransford (Eds.), *Perceiving, acting, and knowing*. Hillsdale, NJ: Erlbaum.

Hansen, W. B., & Altman, I. (1976). Decorating Personal Spaces: A Descriptive Analysis. *Environment and Behavior, 8*, 491-504.

Hillier B., & Hanson J. (1984). *The social logic of space*. Cambridge University Press: Cambridge.

Jones, A. P. (1999). Indoor Air Quality and Health. *Atmospheric Environment, 43*, 4535-4564.

Maslow. A. (1970). *Motivation and personality* (2nd ed). New York: Harper & Row.